SHAME AND GUILT:
Characteristics of the Dependency Cycle

About the Author:

Ernest Kurtz received his Ph.D. in the History of
American Civilization from Harvard University in
1978 and came to the study of history after profes-
sional experience in both religion and psychology.

He has lectured at the Rutgers University Summer
School of Alcohol Studies, and he is currently a
member of the faculty of the Department of History
at the University of Georgia.

SHAME AND GUILT:
Characteristics of the Dependency Cycle
(An Historical Perspective for Professionals)

Ernest Kurtz, Ph.D.

Always, the pioneer

First published, June, 1981

Printed in the United States of America

A list of works referred to or consulted by the author appears at the back of the text. Hazelden expresses its appreciation to those authors and publishers whose materials have been quoted.

TABLE OF CONTENTS

Page

INTRODUCTION
The Lesson of Alcoholics Anonymous

Two distinct experiences — two different ways of feeling "bad" — afflict every alcoholic or addict.* Both can impede recovery. Neither is unique to the alcoholic, but each has a special place in the process of recovery from alcoholism. Alcoholism and its effective treatment, indeed, contribute to our knowledge of the human condition because they reveal so clearly the importance of distinguishing between these two often-confused phenomena. Many hurting people could profit from learning this distinction, but for most alcoholics and addicts, learning and living it become quite literally a matter of life and death. The distinction is between guilt and shame.

*Throughout the text, although in general only the terms "alcohol," "alcoholic," and "alcoholism" will be used, the concept is intended to include all mood-altering chemicals, all chemically dependent people, and all forms of chemical dependency.

Shame differs from guilt. Understanding their difference sheds light on two important realities familiar to anyone who works in alcoholism treatment: how alcoholism differs from other human problems, and why effective therapy for alcoholism must differ from therapies designed to treat other human infirmities. Because guilt and shame differ, the therapies that touch and treat them must also differ.

Some therapies, for some conditions, can afford to ignore the distinction between guilt and shame. In their clients, guilt and shame are so intertwined that confusing the two does not substantially hinder the recovery of full humanity. But such is not the case with the alcoholic. Like any hurting person, the alcoholic suffers *both* guilt and shame. But for the alcoholic, distinguishing between guilt and shame and confronting *each* constructively is necessary not only to attain sobriety but — perhaps more importantly — to maintain ongoing recovery.

Sobriety, the experience of Alcoholics Anonymous teaches us, has two phases: first it must be attained; then it must be maintained. Attaining and maintaining — getting and keeping — sobriety requires different but related emphases. As Bill Wilson (quoting Doctor Bob Smith) told one group of alcoholism professionals: "Honesty gets us sober, but tolerance keeps us sober."[1] The honesty that lies at the heart of the A.A. program forces the distinction between guilt and shame. The tolerance that infuses the A.A. fellowship teaches and enables continuing constructive confrontation with both.

Confronting guilt, though painful, is not difficult. The beginner in Alcoholics Anonymous finds guilt allayed, indeed, by the very concepts of powerlessness and unmanageability that invite him to confront also his shame. The recovering alcoholic finds further help in dealing with guilt in the inventory and amendment Steps (Four, Five, Eight, and Nine) of the A.A. program, which guide directly to guilt's resolution.

The confrontation with shame, although set in motion by A.A.'s First Step, proves more tricky — and, for most, more difficult. Again, the A.A. program — all of it, but especially Steps Two, Six, Seven, and Ten — suggests shame's solution. It is Alcoholics Anonymous as fellowship, however, that makes real this solution; and it is only in the conjunction of A.A. as program and fellowship that the alcoholic can find continuing true therapy for shame.

The impressive success of Alcoholics Anonymous in dealing with alcoholism and addiction flows directly from A.A.'s effectiveness as a therapy for precisely shame.* Other therapies fail, especially over time, because unfaced shame proves much more dangerous to the alcoholic, especially in recovery, than does unresolved guilt. An appreciation of Alcoholics Anonymous as specifically a therapy for shame thus can offer much to those concerned with helping the chemically dependent person truly and at depth.

*This is also why so many other therapies for difficulties far removed from alcoholism — obesity, grief, certain deforming diseases, for example — build their programs on A.A.'s Twelve Steps. The whole "Self-Help Mutual Aid Group Movement" owes its philosophy and most of its modalities to Alcoholics Anonymous.[2]

As should be clear from the preceding portion of the introduction, the exploration of guilt and shame and their significance that follows derives primarily from the author's study and appreciation of the fellowship and program of Alcoholics Anonymous.*

One large significance of Alcoholics Anonymous as a phenomenon in intellectual history consists in the fact that A.A. was the first — and in many ways remains the only — modern therapy to deal directly and effectively with human shame. Other ideas, derived from other sources, have aided and furthered this analysis: I have explored them, and their precise relationship to Alcoholics Anonymous, elsewhere, primarily for scholars of the history of ideas.[3]

Here my intention and effort are to set forth the results of that scholarly investigation in a format accessible to the many and varied people who seek to understand and to help the alcoholic, the addict, the chemically dependent person. I hope and trust that what this presentation lacks in scholarly apparatus and rigor, it gains in utilitarian clarity. On this topic, the test of truth lies not in congruence with academic norms but in resonance with the experience of those who know in the depths of their being the experience of addiction to mood-changing drugs — and the greater experience of ongoing recovery from that addiction.

*The nature of that appreciation and the results of that study are set forth in detail and depth in my book, *Not-God: A History of Alcoholics Anonymous* (Hazelden, 1979). The book is the published version of a Harvard University doctoral dissertation in the History of American Civilization.

PART ONE: DISCOVERING AND RECOGNIZING SHAME

I. DEFINITIONS: EMBARRASSMENT, GUILT AND SHAME

Because of general confusion and wariness about guilt and shame, both terms have recently tended to fall into disuse. "Guilt" seems mainly a legal concept, while the word "shame" is reserved for training children and animals. The reasons behind this confusion and wariness are complex. In briefest outline, modern psychology's distinctions between "rational" and "irrational" guilt, between "true guilt" and "guilty fear," have combined with a psychological age's mistrust of moralism to render most people suspicious of and uncomfortable with the word "guilt" except in contexts narrowly psychiatric or legal. "Shame" suffers from its association with upbringing and helpless dependency: it carries connotations of being "caught" and the implication that a consistently mature person will have no occasion to feel such disgrace.

But that very implication invites probing deeper. "Shame" is tricky, even treacherous: its usual understanding contains a trap. As commonly thought of, "shame" seems a virtual synonym for "embarrassment"; that is, to result from being seen by another. This misunderstanding arises, perhaps, because as children we learn the meaning of "shame" when someone projects it upon us. "You should be ashamed of yourself" is a reproach of public behavior — of something one is seen or caught doing. But the essence of shame consists not in being seen or being caught, but in *what* about one is seen, in *what* one is caught doing. "Embarrassment," then, is not a synonym for shame, but the result of one's shame being seen. "Being seen" or "being caught" are not the essence of shame: we are all seen by others, often and diversely. At times, indeed, we relish being seen: our moments of success and triumph are enhanced by having an audience. "Being seen," then, is not the core even of embarrassment. The heart of embarrassment is that another sees our shame. The sense of shame comes before the sense of being seen — before, then, any advertence to "other."

Shame inheres in us, in ourselves — indeed, literally in our self. "Others," as we shall explore below, are neither the problem in nor the source of shame; rather, others offer the only therapeutic solution for shame. That is why it is so important to distinguish clearly between "embarrassment" and shame.

Both guilt and shame involve feeling "bad" — feeling bad about one's actions (or omissions) in the case of guilt; feeling bad about one's self in shame. There are, in human experience, two different ways of feeling "bad." Each has to do with the boundaries of the human condition. An image may help to clarify the distinction and its point.

To be human is to be surrounded by boundaries: it is somewhat like standing in the middle of a football field. As on a football field, there are two kinds of boundaries: side-lines and end-lines. The side-lines are containing boundaries: to cross them is to "go out of bounds," to do something wrong. The end-lines are goal-lines: the purpose of the game is to attain and to cross them. One feels "bad" (guilty) when one crosses the side-line, the restraining boundary. Feeling "bad" about the goal-line (shame) arises not from crossing it but from *not* crossing it, from failing to attain it.

Guilt, in this image, arises from the violation —
transgression, stepping across — of some limiting boundary;
shame occurs when a goal — an end — is not reached, is
fallen short of. Guilt thus indicates an infraction, a breaking
of the rules; shame, a literal "shortcoming," a lack or defect
of being. The following schema may clarify:

	GUILT	**SHAME**
Results from:	a violation, a transgression, a fault of *doing*	a failure, a falling short, a fault of *being*
	the exercise of power, of control	the lack of power, of control
Results in:	feeling of wrong-doing, sense of wickedness: "not good"	feeling of inadequacy, sense of worthlessness: "no good"

This understanding of guilt and shame suggests four
topics for investigation: (1) how to distinguish between guilt
and shame in actual human experience; (2) the significance
of this distinction for our understanding of the human
condition; (3) the specific qualities of shame that enable its
identification; and (4) the nature of appropriate therapy for
shame. We shall examine each topic in turn, keeping always
in mind that our effort aims to derive effective therapeutic
insight from the actual experience of Alcoholics
Anonymous.

Distinguishing between guilt and shame

The first therapeutic problem to be confronted arises
from the fact that guilt and shame usually come mingled,
together. Although they are distinct experiences, guilt and

shame rarely present themselves separately. Most transgressions, violations of some rule, also involve a failure, falling short of some ideal. If I steal, I not only violate someone else's right; I also fall short of my idea of honesty. The same act (or omission) can thus give rise to *both* guilt and shame: one can feel shame and guilt over the same thing.

The success of Alcoholics Anonymous testifies that in such cases of mingled guilt and shame experienced after a transgression that is also a falling short, distinguishing between guilt and shame and treating first the shame are essential conditions of therapeutic effectiveness. Let us examine, then, how and why.

Making this distinction is not difficult: it can be heard in the accent informing self-blame, in the dual emphasis that inheres in any description of feeling "bad." Guilt reveals itself in self-reproaches that run: how could I have *done that;* what an injurious *thing* to have done; how I hurt *so-and-so;* what a moral lapse that *act* was! Simultaneously, however, shame induces self-reproaches with a very different emphasis: how could *I* have done that; what an *idiot I am;* what a *fool;* how awful and worthless *I am!*[4]

Those who would attempt therapy with persons harboring such mixed feelings — the mixture revealed by the differing accents in "What have I *done?*" and "What have *I* done?" — must be sensitive to both components. Too often, especially in treating alcoholics, therapists settle for the resolution of guilt when it is the confrontation with shame that is the hurting person's deepest need. Indeed, a superficial reading of the A.A. Steps — one that sees the 4th, 5th, 8th, and 9th Steps in isolation from the rest of the Alcoholics Anonymous program — can reinforce this too often tragic error. Those Steps do deal primarily with guilt, but they are but part of the A.A. program. They come embedded, that is to say, in a therapy oriented primarily to the confrontation with shame.

What is this confrontation with shame and how does Alcoholics Anonymous achieve it? The confrontation involves finding, in experiences of shame, truth about the reality of human existence. It means learning, from experiences of falling short, wisdom concerning the meaning of being human. Shame, as its accenting reveals, focuses on the self: it is the perception of not just any lack of failure, but of the deficiency of the self as self, as human being. This is the meaning of shame testifying to flawed being rather than to wrong-doing.

Perhaps surprisingly, despite the depth of self involved in shame's feeling "bad," the sense of shame itself is a good thing — something to be cherished and valued. If this claim that shame is "good" seems strange, reflect for a moment on shame's opposite: indeed, think about the opposites of both guilt and shame. "Guiltless" is clearly a term of praise: to be guiltless, free from guilt, is to be innocent, blameless. "Shameless," on the other hand, is an epithet of condemnation and opprobrium. To be shameless is to be insensible to oneself — insensitive to one's self: one who lacks shame is impudent, brazen, without decency.[5]

Shame, then, despite its negative side that points up failure and falling short, also entails something positive: insight into the reality of the human condition. The experience of shame highlights the essential paradox of the human condition: to be human is to be caught in a contradictory tension between the pull to the unlimited, the more-than-human, and the drag of the merely limited, the less-than-human. There are two difficult concepts here — essential limitation and the human as "middle." We shall examine each of them in turn, carefully, in the light shed by the experience of Alcoholics Anonymous.

II. THE EXPERIENCE AND ACCEPTANCE OF ESSENTIAL LIMITATION

Alcoholics Anonymous teaches as fundamental first truth the ultimate reality of personal essential limitation. "We admitted that we were powerless over alcohol — that our lives had become unmanageable." A.A. addresses itself not to the thing, alcoholism, but to the person, the alcoholic; and the First Step of its program focuses upon the alcoholic as essentially limited. "Powerless . . . unmanageable": the acknowledgement "I am an alcoholic" that is inherent in these admissions accepts as first truth personal essential limitation. The newcomer to Alcoholics Anonymous is thus led to admit, to accept, and to embrace fundamental finitude — essential limitation — as the definition of his alcoholic human condition.

The concept of "*essential* limitation" comes hard: if it poses problems for philosophers, how can it be learned by the lowly alcoholic — indeed, not only learned but inculcated into the very marrow of his being? The program and fellowship of Alcoholics Anonymous accomplish this in several ways, ways that we shall explore throughout the remainder of this booklet. Here, let us focus on but two: the idea of "alcoholic" and the significance of "the first drink."

The two are related. The "alcoholic," A.A. teaches, is one who cannot drink any alcohol safely. There is an essential "not" — an inherent limitation — in the very concept of "alcoholic." This "not" is an essential rather than an accidental limitation, because it applies to the first drink. We all know the gropings of the active alcoholic who realizes that he is in trouble — his staunch efforts to stop drinking before drunkenness, his tortured attempts to determine what is "his limit": two drinks? four beers? only with meals? A.A., in teaching that "the first drink gets the

alcoholic drunk," inculcates that the alcoholic does not
have a limit, he is limited — and this is the meaning of
essential limitation.

To be confronted by one's own essential limitation, to
perceive oneself as essentially limited: these are narrowing,
choking, tightening experiences. We feel these sensations in
our innards, and we struggle against their implications with
all our might. But struggle and might aggravate rather than
alleviate the pain. Although anyone who has felt that pain
can never forget it, the sensation is difficult to name.
Philosophers have called it *Angst* or *angoisse;* in English, the
dreads of "anxiety" and "anguish." All of these terms derive
from the same anxiety source: ANGH, a primitive root the
very sound of which conveys the sense of choked tightness
gasped when something squeezes around one's throat.
Although difficult to name, this sense is all too familiar to
the alcoholic struggling with his addiction — the clutching
feeling of dread that arises from the recognition that one is
out of control. ANGH is the rub of finitude, reminding of
essential limitation.[6]

Alcoholism is an experience of ANGH: it brings home the
realization that to be human is to be essentially limited. The
first reponse to this reminder is shame. The pain of ANGH
arises, indeed, because something else within "being
human" strives to reach beyond limitation and seeks to
impose that one should not be limited — insists, in short,
that any limitation marks the failure of falling short.
Because of the A.A. vision of the human as "not-God," it is
here, on the field of essential limitation, that Alcoholics
Anonymous first wrestles with the alcoholic's shame.

The lesson is unwelcome and difficult; and therefore
Alcoholics Anonymous teaches in several ways this insight
that, because the first truth for the alcoholic is essential
limitation, the first act required for the alcoholic to begin

recovery is the acceptance of essential limitation. Most striking, perhaps, because so often misunderstood, is how A.A. inculcates this truth by applying the insight to itself.

At its very birth, Alcoholics Anonymous departed Oxford Group auspices because the Group, with its heritage of Christian perfectionism as revealed in its emphasis upon "The Four Absolutes," seemed both to demand and to claim too much.[7] Because of this intuition that—at least for alcoholics—the problem of the Oxford Group, as well as one off-putting aspect of all organized religion, was that they claimed to do too much, Alcoholics Anonymous focused attention on its own limitations. Thus, A.A.'s claim that its fellowship and program are "spiritual rather than religious" involves not so much a rejection of religion as a profession of the acceptance of limitation. This understanding is confirmed by another Alcoholics Anonymous axiom, one especially dear to the heart and pen of its only philosopher, William Griffith Wilson. Bill made the point consistently, in many private letters as well as in his published writings, that even as "spiritual," A.A. was but "a kindergarten of the spirit."[8] He intended the image both to ensure A.A.'s own humility, its acceptance of its very real limitations, and to encourage A.A. members to grow in sobriety—and spirituality—in their own individual ways.

The fact of fundamental finitude and the need to accept this essential limitation pervade the fellowship and program of Alcoholics Anonymous. They are clear in the oft-repeated A.A. mottoes, "First Things First" and "One Day at a Time." The emphasis upon accepting limitation infuses A.A.'s own description of "How It Works" from the "Rarely" that opens that key fifth chapter of its Big Book, through the "tried to" that lies at the heart of its Twelfth Step, to its concluding qualification of its promise of "progress rather than ... perfection."[9]

Honesty concerning essential limitation is therefore the core of Alcoholics Anonymous. Such honesty thus becomes both the price and the reward, both the process and the purpose, of the A.A. member's First Step acceptance of himself as "powerless over alcohol." In a way suggestive of the psychoanalytic contract, Alcoholics Anonymous has intuited the existential truth that accepting the reality of self-as-feared may be an essential pre-condition of finding the reality of self-as-is.

PART TWO: CONFRONTING SHAME

I. SHAME AND THE MEANING OF BEING HUMAN

We have seen that by its own example, as well as by its core message, Alcoholics Anonymous teaches its members that there is a wholeness in limitation. This understanding echoes an ancient tradition of wisdom, which saw being human as being caught in the middle, containing a contradiction. To be human, according to this tradition, means to sustain the tension of always being pulled in two opposite directions: to be more than human and to be less than human.[10]

This vision has haunted many thinkers. Two very different philosophers, whose thoughts span centuries, can clarify its meaning for us; for—if we take care to understand them correctly—their insights anticipate two descriptions of alcoholic experience that may be heard detailed at virtually any meeting of Alcoholics Anonymous. Their vision posits an image: man, located on the scale of reality between "beast" and "angel," contains within himself both "beast" and "angel." To be human, then, is to experience from within the contradictory pulls to be both angel and beast, both more and less than merely human. Because of these contradictory pulls, to be human is to live in a tension: because one is pulled to both, one can exclusively attain neither. Yet the tension pinches and strains; and some humans strive to resolve it by becoming only one or the other, beast or angel.

Over three hundred years ago, the French mathematician and mystic Blaise Pascal observed of one such effort: "He who would be an angel becomes a beast."[11] That is, the attempt to be more than human leads to being less than human. Early in the present century, the Spanish-born, Harvard philosopher George Santayana utilized the same image to make its complementary point: "It is necessary to become a beast if one is ever to be a spirit."[12] That is, to attain the heights of human existence, one must also touch its depths.

Together, these understandings and their point—as both angel and beast, one cannot be only either — embrace the core perception and process of Alcoholics Anonymous. In the A.A. understanding that can be heard, paraphrased, at any A.A. meeting, the alcoholic drank in the attempt or claim to be one or the other, angel or beast; the essence of sobriety resides in the acceptance that one is both—that because one can be only both, the effort to be only one or the other dooms one to insatiable frustration.

This vision of the human as both angel and beast thus captures well the descriptions of drinking experience heard within Alcoholics Anonymous—the vivid portrayal of the heights and the depths reached for and even attained, only to have their opposites relentlessly and inevitably recur. This understanding of the meaning of being human posits and emphasizes an essential incongruity—an inherent conflict, contradiction, antinomy—at the very core of the human condition. Both the theme and its inherent incongruity have been explored in detail by several recent writers who, although they have not looked directly at the alcoholic, have sensitively delineated the painful paradox of human aspiration conjoined with human finitude, human hope subverted by human limitation.

Yet the paradox need not be only painful. One of its modern students, the anthropologist Ernest Becker in his Pulitzer prize-winning study of *The Denial of Death,* has captured its essence in a striking phrase that not only can further our appreciation of the paradox but that can reveal the humor that lies on the other side of its pain. And that insight into humor can deepen our understanding of Alcoholics Anonymous as therapy for shame. In Becker's vivid and memorable image, to be human is to be "a god who shits."[13]

The humor of being human

Humor, in a definition that reflects itself, "arises from the perception of the juxtaposition of incongruity." We find funny the placing together of things that do not belong together: the portly, top-hatted, distinguishedly pompous gentleman slipping on a banana peel, for example. Humor and laughter may, of course, be aggressive and even cruel—especially when the other is objectified rather than identified with. But when humor's incongruity is inherent—a reflection of the essential contradiction of being human with which one identifies—there can be no more healing, whole-ing, experience than the laughter that marks identifying acceptance of that paradoxical incongruity.[14]

Such laughter characterizes meetings of Alcoholics Anonymous, revealing much about A.A.'s healing power. The stories told at these meetings exquisitely demonstrate the essential incongruity of the human condition, the humor inherent in being human.

I'd sit up all night, just about, watching the late
late *late* movies, tears streaming down my face,
thinking "Yes, that's how life really is, loveless and
tragic"; and I'd toast each sad revelation with
another warming swallow of booze. During the
breaks I'd go out to the kitchen to get more ice,
and passing the hall mirror I'd look soulfully at my
image in it—with immense, enormous self-pity, but
with no realization at all that the bleary-eyed,
puffy, unshaven condition of my face and its
booze-stinking breath just might have something
to do with my being unloved.

Or:

When I first came around A.A., someone suggested
that I get down on my knees each morning and ask
for help to not take a drink that day. Well, I
resented that! *Me,* kneel down and ask for help?
No way...so I didn't come back, for a while.
Instead I went back to drinking, my usual pattern,
until one morning it came to me. There I was, in
my accustomed morning position, kneeling on the
cold tile of my bathroom floor with my arms
wrapped around the toilet heaving my guts out.
The thought crossed my mind that it wasn't the
kneeling or the asking for help that bothered
me—after all, that's just what I was doing! It was
that those A.A.'s wanted me to do it on a warm,
carpeted floor with a serene stomach! And if *that*
was what bothered me, maybe they were right and
I *was* "sick," and so I decided to give you folks
another try.

Such humor and the laughter that greets it are never
aimed at others as objects, but at the contradictions within
self illuminated by the human experience described. A.A.

laughter expresses appreciation of the insights into self garnered from the experience of others with whom one identifies. Thus, humor within Alcoholics Anonymous witnesses to A.A. members' acceptance of the paradoxical nature of the human condition as not-God: as essentially limited but inherently striving for the unlimited. In attempting and claiming to attain transcendence by their use of alcohol, alcoholics come to touch—even to wallow in—the depths of their own finitude.

Recognizing the incongruity between that endeavor and its result frees from both. Such humor is neither veiled aggression nor mere compensation; it rather manifests the central animus of A.A.'s theory of personality and of human nature. The human as not-God means that the essence of being human resides in the human condition's conjunction of infinite thirst with essentially limited capacity. Acceptance of this reality comes easily to the alcoholic who understands his alcoholism; the phenomenon of alcoholism replicates the essence of the human condition.[15]

II. TWO COROLLARIES OF SHAME: LIMITED CONTROL AND LIMITED DEPENDENCE

Its own example in accepting limitation and the gift of healing humor that its meetings offer are not the only ways in which Alcoholics Anonymous inculcates in its members the acceptance of essential limitation that enables constructive confrontation with shame. Its insight into the human condition furnishes A.A. with another understanding, one that illuminates both its diagnosis of and its therapy for the alcoholic. As Bill Wilson never tired of reminding, "the alcoholic is an all-or-nothing person."[16] The futility of this effort to deny the essential some-ness of the human experience manifests itself in especially two areas—control and dependence.

In the A.A. understanding, the drinking alcoholic drinks alcohol in an effort to achieve control—*absolute* control—over his feelings and environment; yet his drinking itself is absolutely out of control. Similarly, the drinking alcoholic denies all dependence. He drinks in an attempt to deny dependence upon others, upon anything outside himself; but his dependence upon alcohol itself has become absolute. The alcoholic's problem, then, involves the demand for absolute control and the claim to be absolutely independent. A.A. as therapy attacks this double problem in a twofold way. First, the alcoholic is confronted with the facts that, so far as alcohol is concerned, he is absolutely out of control and absolutely dependent. Then, when this reality (contained in the very concept "alcoholic") has been accepted by the admission of "powerlessness over alcohol," Alcoholics Anonymous prescribes limited control and limited dependence.

An image, an ancient posture, clarifies the relationship between the human-as-middle and its corollaries of limited control and limited dependence. In the original, privately published version of A.A.'s Twelve Steps, the Seventh Step opened with the phrase: "Humbly on our knees..."[17] Kneeling, the Pietist posture, is a middle position—half-way between standing upright and lying flat. A.A.'s interpretation of the alcoholic condition may be conceptualized around this image. The alcoholic is one who, in his claim to absolute independence and absolute control over alcohol, insists on trying to stand unaided, only to inevitably fall flat on his face—often literally in the gutter. To the alcoholic lying prone, Alcoholics Anonymous suggests: "Get *up* on your knees—you can do something, but not everything." Later, in the alcoholic's progress toward sobriety, A.A. often has occasion to temper tendencies to grandiosity with a similar suggestion: "Get *down* on your knees — you can do something, but not everything." A.A.'s insight into the middleness of the human condition—its limited control and limited dependence—linchpins its total approach to the alcoholic, drinking or sober.

The emphasis on control as limited, as neither absolute nor to be abdicated, pervades the A.A. program. "You can do something, but not everything": A.A. members are warned against promising "never to drink again." They learn, rather, "not to take the first drink, one day at a time." They learn to pick up the telephone instead of the bottle. They are encouraged to attend A.A. meetings, which they can do, rather than to avoid all contact with alcohol, which they cannot do. The A.A. sense of limited control is admirably summed up in its famed "Serenity Prayer": "God grant me the serenity to accept the things I cannot change, the courage to change the things I can, and the wisdom to know the difference."

The "can" and "cannot" of the Serenity Prayer well inculcate the concepts of limited control and limited dependence. They also clarify the depth of the dedication of Alcoholics Anonymous to human freedom. In the A.A. understanding, alcoholism is an obsessive-compulsive malady; the active alcoholic is one who *must* drink, who cannot not-drink. Therefore the alcoholic who joins the A.A. fellowship and embraces its program does not thereby surrender his freedom to drink; rather, he gains the freedom to not-drink — no small liberation for one obsessively-compulsively addicted to alcohol. Within Alcoholics Anonymous, indeed, the passage from "mere dryness" to "true sobriety" consists precisely in the change of perception — perspective — by which the A.A. member moves from interpreting his situation as the prohibition, "I cannot drink" to understanding its deeper reality as the joyous affirmation, "I *can* not-drink."

For the alcoholic, freedom consists in *not* drinking; and, as
any truly sober A.A. member will readily testify, there is a
world of difference between the necessary first stage of
accepting the limitation "I cannot drink" and embracing the
freedom of the happy new reality "I *can* not-drink." A.A.'s
success derives in no small part from the fact that it is the
only therapy for alcoholics that contains a philosophy that
embraces and teaches such an understanding of the reality
of human freedom.

"Limited control," however, is but one side of the coin of
human freedom: its obverse face reveals limited
dependence. Here, the philosophy of Alcoholics Anonymous
again subtly challenges a frequent, modern assumption.
Other therapies approach the alcoholic from a point of view
that sees all dependence—but especially the essential
dependence that binds the alcoholic to his chemical—as
humiliating and dehumanizing. They tell the alcoholic that
maturity—becoming fully human—involves overcoming all ·
such dependencies. Diagnosing alcoholism, virtually all
modern therapies proclaim that the alcoholic's problem is
"dependence on alcohol," and they endeavor to break the
alcoholic's dependence.

The larger-wisdomed insight of Alcoholics Anonymous
does not exactly contradict this understanding. Indeed, A.A.
agrees with and accepts this diagnosis that the alcoholic's
problem is "dependence on alcohol." But Alcoholics
Anonymous—and this is one important key to its
success—locates the definition's deeper truth by shifting its
implicit emphasis. A.A. interprets the experience of its
members as revealing that the alcoholic's problem is not
"*dependence* on alcohol," but "dependence on *alcohol*." To
be human, to be essentially limited, Alcoholics Anonymous
insists, is to *be* essentially dependent. The alcoholic's
choice—the *human* choice—lies not between dependence

and independence, but between that upon which one will acknowledge dependence — a less than human substance such as alcohol within oneself, or a more than individual reality that remains essentially outside — beyond — the self.

We shall return to this topic of the alcoholic's "dependence" below, in exploring the precise nature and style of the limited dependence that Alcoholics Anonymous proposes as a therapy for shame because it enhances the alcoholic's humanity. Before turning directly to that focus on therapy, however, it is necessary to examine certain characteristics of shame that render it appropriate for the therapy of Alcoholics Anonymous.

III. THE QUALITIES OF SHAME

We seem, perhaps, to have come a long way, a far distance, from our stated topic of shame and guilt. Yet have we? Shame, recall, arises from the feeling of failure, from the sense of falling short. But, in the Alcoholics Anonymous understanding of the human condition, to be human *is* to fall short. Any therapy that would aid the alcoholic, then, must confront the inevitability of falling short that the alcoholic as "all-or-nothing person" sought to avoid or to deny by his use of alcohol.

How is this to be done? The confrontation with shame, the acceptance of self as essentially limited, involves two stages: (1) recognizing shame for what it is, and especially its distinction from guilt; (2) finding and applying the mode of therapy that enables one to live constructively with one's own essential limitation and therefore with that positive shame without which one becomes "shameless." We turn then, first, to the qualities that characterize shame: avenues that open to touching shame and therefore to embracing one's own essential limitation.

Three characteristics of shame—or better, of its occasion—both aid in distinguishing shame from guilt and illuminate the nature of the essential limitation that lies at the core of being human. Guilt, recall, arises from the violation of some restraining boundry: it characteristically has to do with moral transgression, results from a voluntary act, and tends to be proportionate to the gravity of the offense committed. Shame, in contrast, can be recognized because it may be evoked by a non-moral lapse, may arise for an involuntary act, and tends to be magnified by the very triviality of its stimulus.

The non-moral

Shame may arise from either a moral or a non-moral lapse. For some, the possibility of non-moral shame provides the key to understanding its distinction from guilt. Two cases of non-moral shame are especially relevant in the present context: failure in love and the failure of sickness.

Perhaps the most common source of non-moral shame is disappointment or frustration, and specifically disappointment in love. One who seeks to win another's love, and fails, suffers not the guilt of moral transgression but the constricted hollowness of felt inadequacy. Experiences of defeat, disappointment, frustration, or failure evoke shame. Guilt, as transgression, always involves aggression: one feels guilty about the aggression. Shame, although it may involve an aspect of aggression, arises over the attempt's failure rather than over the attempt itself.[18]

Both the "disease-concept of alcoholism" and A.A.'s emphasis on alcoholism as "malady" also serve to bring the alcoholic's drinking under the heading of shame.[19] To be ill is not to transgress, but to fall short. One large contribution of Alcoholics Anonymous, no less than of modern medical research, has been to remove alcoholism from moral categories. This removal, of course, is more easily claimed than achieved; but distinguishing between guilt and shame can help further that achievement.

The alcoholic who knows from experience that he should not drink but who obsessively-compulsively does drink will of course and inevitably feel "bad." If he knows only the category of guilt, he cannot help but judge his drinking to be somehow a moral transgression. Learning the disease concept, however, enables transcending guilt by inviting confrontation with shame. A.A.'s contribution here is to distinguish clearly between the guilty feeling of wickedness and the shamed sense of worthlessness. The experience of Alcoholics Anonymous teaches that the alcoholic's key problem is not that he is wicked, but that he feels worthless. A.A. therapy treats first, then, not guilt but shame.

The involuntary

The concept of disease and the experience of many diversely sick people who are ashamed of their illnesses also clarify the second characteristic of occasions of specifically shame—their involuntariness.* That shame arises involuntarily—from incapacity, the failure of choice—should be clear from its very concept as outlined near the beginning of this paper. Guilt implies choice; haggling over guilt often focuses upon the question of how free was the choice, but the fact of choice is assumed. Shame, on the other hand, occurs over a falling short, a

---

* The most recent development in this field has been the extension of this philosophy—A.A. philosophy—to the terminally ill, especially to those dying of cancer.

missing of the mark, a failure of powers.* Involuntariness is
a necessary concomitant of shame's focus upon the
deficiency of self. The core of the pain in shame arises from
the failure of choice, of will. An example may clarify. One
seduced into adultery might feel both guilt and shame: guilt
over the violation of the marriage promise; shame at falling
short of the marriage ideal. The man who finds himself
sexually impotent with a woman he loves will feel
predominantly shame: the question of morality does not
enter, and—at least in his conscious mind—his sexual
disability is anything but voluntary.

When an alcoholic says "Why?": "Why do I drink (or do
x)—I know I don't want to!" the therapist imbued with the
philosophy of Alcoholics Anonymous knows better than to
try to probe and to prove that he really did want to. The
A.A. answer, accepting involuntariness, is simple. "You
didn't want to, but you did. You did because you are an
alcoholic. That is what an alcoholic is: one who drinks when
he doesn't want to. The answer to 'Why' lies not in your will,
but in the fact that you are an alcoholic."

Experiences of shame are valuable because, by their
involuntariness, they teach about the limitation of human
will. The alcoholic cannot will to not-drink any more than
the insomniac can will to fall asleep. The example is exact;
for, in both cases, one can will the means, but any attempt
directly to will the end proves self-defeating. There are, it
seems, two distinct kinds of "will," two different realms in
which human will operates. In some matters, will chooses to

* A "missing of the mark": those familiar with ancient languages
or theological thought may recognize the concept of hamartia—an
ancient term for "sin." The parallel is a rich one, and I wish here
to express gratitude to Gordon Grimm and Rock Stack of
Hazelden's Clinical Pastoral Education Department for offering
the opportunity to discover and explore it.

move in a certain direction; in others, will chooses to possess a particular object. Problems arise when we attempt to apply the will of the second realm—the utilitarian will that chooses objects—to those portions of life that, because they are directions or orientations, wilt or even vanish under such coercion.

Let me try to clarify by suggesting a few other examples, probably familiar to anyone, of this distinction: I can will knowledge, but not wisdom; submission, but not humility; self-assertion, but not courage; congratulations, but not admiration; religiosity, but not faith; reading, but not understanding; physical nearness, but not emotional closeness; dryness, but not sobriety.*

Because shame often arises from the failure of the effort to will what cannot be willed, experiences of shame contain an important lesson for the alcoholic. To know shame is to realize that certain things—the realm of orientation and direction, as in the examples above—fall beyond the scope of the utilitarian will that chooses objects. This realization is important because a major source of anxiety is the effort to will what cannot be willed. The alcoholic seeks chemical relief from such anxiety because drugs—for example, alcohol—offer the illusion of healing this split between the will and its impossible goal. The recovering alcoholic knows that such chemical pacification is "illusion," but its remembered attractiveness can haunt one pinched by the pain of anxiety. Insofar, then, as will and its failure enter

* Several of these examples, and the ideas in this and the following paragraph, have been suggested and are treated at greater depth in two essays by Leslie H. Farber: "Thinking About Will" and "Will and Anxiety," in <u>Lying, Despair, Jealousy, Envy, Sex, Suicide, Drugs, and the Good Life</u> (New York: 1976), pp. 3-34.

into the alcoholic's problem, experiences of shame offer a potent reminder of the essential limitation of will with which the alcoholic—like any human—must learn to live. The involuntary quality of shame thus teaches important lessons about the nature of sobriety and serenity.

The trivial

The third and final characteristic of shame to be examined is the apparent disproportion in shame that renders it literally so monstrous an experience. Usually, the depth and extent of guilt correlate with the gravity of the offense: the more serious the transgression, the greater the guilt. Shame, on the contrary, tends to be triggered by the most trivial of stimuli, by some seemingly small and even picayune detail. Such details, precisely as trivial, reveal most unmistakably the deficiency of self as self rather than as violator of some abstract code. The employee who embezzled a thousand dollars, when he comes to doing his Eighth and Ninth Steps, tends to feel predominantly guilt. The person who has cadged quarters off his co-workers' desks, who has habitually ignored the office coffee-pot's plea for coin contributions, will feel more shame than guilt. If a sensitive therapist can tap that shame, can touch that triviality, he will more acutely and thoroughly help one contemplating A.A.'s Eighth and Ninth Steps to confront himself as he is. The trivial invites examining "What kind of person am I to have done that?" The more trivial the "that," the more readily the emphasis moves to "person."[20]

The disproportion that tends to inhere in shame—its tendency to be greater according as its stimulus is smaller—reveals another intriguing facet of shame that renders it especially appropriate for the therapy of Alcoholics Anonymous. In one sense, albeit not technically, shame is addictive. The disproportion inherent in it serves to magnify shame, for one becomes ashamed at the very inappropriateness of one's reaction, and therefore ashamed of shame itself. Perhaps because of this insatiable quality in shame over the trivial, it is upon the disproportion inherent in experiences of shame that the program of Alcoholics Anonymous fastens in turning shame to therapeutically constructive use.

Alcoholics Anonymous locates the "root of [the alcoholic's] troubles" in the selfishness of "self-centeredness" — in pride.[21] The drinking alcoholic tends to deem himself exceptional, different, special; and this tendency does not suddenly cease in early sobriety. Thus, one trap for the newly recovering alcoholic, freshly enthusiastic about his A.A. program, lies in the temptation to judge himself, as he reviews his personal history of alcoholism, especially "wicked." As one therapist has acutely observed of both drinking and sober alcoholics: "The alcoholic's problem is not that he feels, 'I am a worm,' nor even that he feels, 'I am very special.' The main obstacle to therapy is that the alcoholic feels, 'I am a very special worm.'" Admittedly, the telling of stories at A.A. meetings can on occasion exacerbate this problem by degenerating into "Can you top this?" competitions. Yet as usually and properly used, the telling of stories at A.A. meetings and especially the Fifth Step of the A.A. program provides direct therapy for the "very special worm" trap.

"Admitted to God, to ourselves, and to another human being, the exact nature of our wrongs." Such confession is, of course, ancient religious practice. Yet within Alcoholics Anonymous as within its parent Oxford Group, this practice ministers to shame more than to guilt. The essential point was already clear in the Oxford Group understanding: "This sharing leads to the discovery that sins we thought were so bad are quite run-of-the-mill. The regard of one's sins as particularly awful is a vicious form of pride that is overcome by sharing."[22] A.A.'s Fifth Step, like its practice of story-telling, serves to inculcate a similar awareness: the alcoholic, as essentially limited not-God, is very ordinary. This is why A.A.'s Fifth Step is presented as ending "the old pangs of anxious apartness" and beginning the alcoholic's "emergence from isolation."[23]

IV. SHAME, EXPOSURE, DENIAL, AND HIDING

Because of the disproportion inherent in shame, because shame's stimulus is so often trivial and shame itself therefore usually so surprising, experiences of shame are experiences of exposure. Experiences of shame throw a flooding and searching light on what and who we are, painfully uncovering unrecognized aspects of personality. Exposure—*exposure to oneself*—lies at the heart of shame. The root meaning of the word "shame" implies this process: to uncover, to expose, to wound. Experiences of shame are thus experiences of the exposure of peculiarly sensitive, intimate, vulnerable aspects of the self. The exposure may be to others; but, whether others are involved or not, the significant exposure is always to one's own eyes. An incident described by Somerset Maugham in his study *Of Human Bondage* vividly penetrates to the essence of shame as the exposure to oneself of one's own weakness.[24]

The protagonist in the story, Philip, as a new boy at school, was ragged by his classmates who demanded to see his clubfoot. Despite his almost obsequious desire for friendship, Philip adamantly refused to show his handicap. Finally, one night, a group of boys attacked Philip in his bed, and the school bully twisted his arm until Philip stuck his leg out of the bed to let them see his deformity. The boys then laughed and left.

> Philip . . . got his teeth in the pillow so that his sobbing should be inaudible. He was not crying for the pain they had caused him, nor for the humiliation he had suffered when they looked at his foot, but with rage at himself because, unable to stand the torture, he had put out his foot on his own accord.

Exposure to others was less painful to Philip than the exposure to himself of his own weakness.

Alcoholism—indeed, addictive dependency upon any psychoactive chemical—often arises from and usually is connected with the effort to conceal such weakness, to prevent its exposure to oneself. The alcoholic or addict uses his chemical in order to hide, and especially to hide from himself. The endeavor to hide reveals that the critical problem underlying such behavior is shame.[25]

Guilt moves to solving problems; shame leads to hiding feelings. "Wanting to be absolved of guilt is not the addict's problem." Usually, the addicted person within himself is pleading passionately to be able to feel guilty. Guilt-oriented therapies, however sophisticated, fail because the addict or alcoholic cannot "mend his ways" or, by willing it, "grow up." He must maintain his addiction precisely to conceal his unendurable shame from himself. Any interference with his chemical dependency threatens to reveal that shame and therefore becomes "a primary survival threat." In any case in which the avoidance of pain—the existential pain of shame—plays a basic part in the organization and maintenance of the psychopathology, effective therapy must address itself first to the existential nature of that pain and shame.

This is one reason why effective treatment for the alcoholic involves *caring* rather than *curing*. The therapy of Alcoholics Anonymous utilizes the realization that to induce—or, more exactly, to allow—humiliation can be an important initial therapeutic goal. The informal format of A.A. meetings, their atmosphere of badinage and humorous, loving confrontation, is well-designed to achieve this goal.

An image may help to clarify A.A.'s style as a therapy for shame. Any hurting person who seeks help brings to therapy a tiny, flickering flame of self-respect. Classic, guilt-oriented therapies strive to nourish that tiny glimmer, to enlarge self-respect. The initial response of Alcoholics Anonymous is different. The newcomer who leads from self-respect meets with caring confrontation: he is offered, for example, a carefully half-filled cup of coffee. Such confrontation of lingering denial invites the hesitant newcomer both to acknowledge the fact of his shakes and to realize that the coffee-server who recognizes the shakes accepts them — and him. The message is less "It's okay" than "It's tough, but I've been there too." More stubborn cases may, in time be told: "Take the cotton out of your ears and put it in your mouth!" Any flicker of self-respect that reveals denial of the felt-worthlessness of shame is gently quashed rather than nourished within A.A. Why? Because A.A. experience testifies that, until that denial is shattered, its own constructive therapy cannot be effective. The alcoholic must confront self-as-feared if he is ever to find the reality of self-as-is.

The characteristic defense of alcoholics is denial—the defense against which the shared honesty of mutual vulnerability openly acknowledged (the core dynamic of A.A. therapy) so effectively operates. Denial involves the hiding of felt-inadequacy of being. Shame, as herein explained, relates so intimately to "denial" because it results

not merely from a "sense of failure," but from a sense of
essential failure—failure as a human being, the failure of
existence. This understanding captures, I believe, the insight
of Dr. Harry Tiebout in his early classic psychiatric
exploration of the therapeutic dynamic operative in
Alcoholics Anonymous.[26] Tiebout distinguished between
"compliance," which he saw as worse than useless because
it obscured the obsessive-compulsive nature of alcoholism,
and "surrender,"which he presented as the key to the
therapeutic process of recovery. Tiebout's "compliance"
may be understood as motivated by guilt: "surrender," as
enabled by the alcoholic's acceptance of his shame.

Denial, Tiebout realized, could continue despite
acknowledgment of—despite even attempts at reparation
for—guilt. Guilt may even be a defense against confronting
and accepting what is denied, as when the alcoholic accepts
responsibility for what he has done when drinking as
preferable to admitting that the drinking itself was beyond
his control. Real guilt fears punishment and tries to escape
it. The shamed person, on the other hand, for example the
alcoholic just described, seeks and embraces
punishment—even by admitting "guilt"—as a confirmation
aiding denial of what is most deeply feared: his own failure
of being, his sense of having failed as a human being.

PART THREE: THERAPY FOR SHAME

I. NEEDING OTHERS

In order to get beyond this hiding, in order to transcend
this denial, in order to succeed as a human being, the
alcoholic needs others. Despite the far too common
misunderstanding that has confused shame with

"embarrassment," "others" are not the problem in shame, but the solution.

Because of their essential limitation, human beings have needs. The denial of essential limitation usually manifests itself not directly, but in the denial of need. The alcoholic's denial of need is twofold: his denial of his need for alcohol blends into and intertwines with his denial of his need for others. Early in the process of alcoholism, the alcoholic denies that it is his unmet because insatiable need for others that leads him to seek comfort or excitement in alcohol. "A few drinks" become more important than the people at a party, for example, as alcohol becomes a surer source of satisfaction than human interaction. Later in the process, after a few failures of "I can stop whenever I want to" (denial of the need for alcohol) the denial becomes again of the need for others: "Just leave me alone—I can lick this thing by myself."

Alcoholics Anonymous enables and promotes recovery from alcoholism by breaking through these twin denials of need. As fellowship, A.A. invites the alcoholic to discover his own need for others by being the one place where the alcoholic himself is needed, and needed precisely and only as alcoholic. This leads to self-identification as "alcoholic," and thus to admission of the need for alcohol. As program, A.A. builds on the admission of the need for alcohol—"I am an alcoholic"—ever deepening awareness of one's need for others: the Twelve Steps of the program of Alcoholics Anonymous begin with the word "We," and A.A. ever emphasizes that it is "fellowship" as well as "program." Thus, the vicious circle of denial of need—for alcohol and for others—is broken and replaced by a twofold, mutually enhancing admission of need.

The "need for others" is, of course, the most famous facet of Alcoholics Anonymous. Usually, those outside A.A.

regard it condescendingly and deprecatingly. It is interpreted away as "the substituting of a social dependence for a drug dependence";[27] or as "accepting the emotional immaturity of alcoholics and supplying a crutch for it."[28] Yet some independent observers have also recognized positive aspects in the need for others that is taught by Alcoholics Anonymous. One psychiatrist, for example, has located the reason for A.A.'s success in this approach, which—as opposed to some mere disease concept of alcoholism—inculcates in the alcoholic and many who would help him the "understanding that human involvement is needed."[29] Alcoholics Anonymous itself, of course, faithful to its Tenth Tradition, remains explicitly silent in the midst of this controversy. A.A. simply performs its chosen task—helping alcoholics get and stay sober—and, because of its familiarity with the treacheries of hiding and denial, even encourages utilizing rather than analyzing its program and fellowship.

If one is struggling to get or to stay sober, "utilize, don't analyze" is appropriate advice: if a person can do only one *or* the other, putting A.A. into practice in one's life is far more important than understanding the depths of its wisdom. Yet that maxim is not applied even by Alcoholics Anonymous to those who can do both. Bill Wilson himself set this example in writing *Twelve Steps and Twelve Traditions,* a book that represents his own analysis of the A.A. program and fellowship. Especially those who, like Bill, thirst in their sobriety to help alcoholics and who indeed build their sobriety on that worthy work can perhaps benefit—both themselves and others—by plunging deeper. The nature of Alcoholics Anonymous as a therapy for shame seems one such helpful plunge. What follows, then, attempts to explore, for those interested, both "How" and "Why" A.A. works as a therapy for shame.

II. SHAME, OBJECTIVITY, AND CARING

In dealing with shame, others are not the problem, but the solution. Both guilt and shame are characterized by "shoulds," but it is the "should" of guilt that comes from outside, from rules made by others. The "should" of shame arises from within, from the nature of the human as essentially limited, yet craving infinity. Another way of stating this is to observe that guilt is objective; shame, subjective. Because it comes in some way from outside, guilt arises objectively: the line that is crossed, the rule that is broken, has objective existence outside oneself. Shame, in contrast, may be thought of as a more subjective experience: the goal fallen short of, the self-ideal that quests and claims unlimitedness, is a part of one's own nature and being. Because of this difference, shame cannot be healed—or even treated—"objectively."

A funny thing about the modern world in which we live: the term "objective" tends to have a good connotation; the term "subjective," to be pejorative. "Objectivity" is a praiseworthy goal; to speak "objectively" is to require credence; calling someone's work or presentation "objective" is to praise it. The parallel terms "subjectivity," "subjectively," and "subjective" are, on the contrary, put-downs. One hears before them "merely," and the implication of flaw and error. We live in a world, indeed, in which "objective" equates with *real,* whereas "subjective" is taken to mean false, unreal, imaginary.

Objectivity is especially desired and valued in the medical—curing—model. We need think no further than the example of the surgeon. Surgeons do not operate on their own family members, on persons with whom they have a caring relationship. Further, even the ordinary patient's body is so prepared and draped for surgery that his or her personhood and individuality are concealed insofar as possible. Everything about the aura, ritual, and procedures of the operating theater is designed to enable the surgeon to perform his skill upon a body rather than upon a person.

In dealing with things as do the physical sciences, or in applying the curing model to human bodies as does medical science, "objectivity" is an obvious virtue. Objects are "out there": how the perceiver relates to them does not make a difference to them. As for the perceiver, "objectivity" enhances his observations of and actions upon objects. But applied to human beings *as* human beings, as persons who are also subjects, the subject-object model with its demand for "objectivity" is vain and doomed to failure. Thinking in terms of subject-object renders others "they" — necessarily apart from and over-against the self. Such a result, indeed such an effort, inevitably distorts: human phenomena are never *merely* objects. In dealing with human phenomena, that is to say, the flaw of "mereness" inheres in objectivity rather than in subjectivity.

Accepting persons as ends-in-themselves, the Kantian imperative, is impossible in a Cartesian world of subject-object relationships. Such acceptance of persons as persons becomes possible only in a world-view that transcends the subject-object dichotomy—a world in which human relationships can be reciprocal and mutual because the subjectivity, the personhood, of each individual is accepted as first truth. Alcoholics Anonymous is not the only modern entity to postulate such a vision, such a reality, such a model of caring. Yet it is specifically the A.A. world-view that concerns us here, and therefore it is the understanding of human relationships that is witnessed to by the experience of Alcoholics Anonymous that we shall examine in this exploration of therapy for shame.

III. COMPLEMENTARITY AND THE MUTUALITIES THAT HEAL SHAME

Within Alcoholics Anonymous, human relationships are characterized by complementarity and mutuality. "Complementarity" means that individuals *fit into* each other, thus enhancing each other rather than diminishing self or others. In such relationships, each is to each other according to the needs of both. "Mutuality" underlines this back-and-forth-ness: the two-way, reciprocal nature of human relationships that are truly human.

Such relationships furnish the invitation and the opportunity to grow and to expand; they are, indeed, the only way to grow as human. As one profound student of the phenomenon of shame has observed:

> The ability to enter into relations of intimacy
> and mutuality opens the way to experiences in
> which the self expands beyond its own limitations
> in depth of feeling, understanding, and insight.
> One's own identity may be not weakened, but
> strengthened by the meaning one has for others...
> and by respect for these other persons as distinct
> individuals.

> This experience involves the risk of trusting
> oneself to other persons instead of regarding them
> in object, status, or audience relations. It also
> means not allowing disappointment in response
> from another person to lead to a denial of the
> expectation and possibility of love...A person who
> is unable to love cannot reveal himself.[30]

Members of Alcoholics Anonymous achieve this ability and experience—this vision of complementary mutuality—by deriving their awareness of their need for others from the fundamental realization that they, as alcoholic, are not God. This realization is not merely privative, the recognition of a lack. The need for others bridges to a positive existence. A.A. members accept themselves not only as not God, but as not-God: they find a positive identity in their essential limitation. The identification, "I am an alcoholic," is spoken as a joyous affirmation within Alcoholics Anonymous.

Other human beings, and most patently other alcoholics—the others most needed by recovering alcoholics—are clearly also essentially limited and therefore also not God. There is, then, an essential limitation on how those others are needed. The first thing known about these others is that they also need others: thus the foundation for mutuality is established.

Making a difference

It is this perception and acceptance of mutuality that enables transcending the "self-centeredness" that members of Alcoholics Anonymous understand to be "the root of our troubles." The mutualities that Alcoholics Anonymous teaches, enables, and lives out are especially three: they involve making a difference, honesty and dependence.

The ability to make a difference is a deeply basic human need; indeed, Alcoholics Anonymous founded its fellowship upon this vital need. Recall A.A.'s origins: Bill Wilson's six-month failure to help any alcoholic until, in Akron on Mothers' Day of 1935, he sought out Doctor Bob Smith for what Bob, as an alcoholic, could give him. Perhaps an even more significant moment occurred at the bedside of the alcoholic who was to become "A.A. Number Three." Wilson and Smith told Bill D. that talking with him was the only way they could stay sober. Bill D. believed them, and therefore he listened:

All the other people that had talked to me
wanted to help *me*, and my pride prevented me
from listening to them, and caused only
resentment on my part, but I felt as if I would be a
real stinker if I did not listen to a couple of fellows
for a short time, if that would cure *them*.[31]

Many later therapists have shared the same insight. The
psychoanalyst R.D. Laing, for example, has criticized the
classic therapeutic approach as defective precisely because
of the model that classic therapists present: "A prototype of
the other as giver but not receiver...tends to generate in self
a sense of failure...Frustration becomes depair when the
person begins to question his own capacity to 'mean'
anything to anyone."[32] Elsewhere, Laing goes further,
suggesting explicitly that the sense of being "not able to
make a difference" issues in shame and despair rather than
guilt: "the person experiences, not the absence of the
presence of the other, but the absence of his own presence
as other for the other."[33]

To appreciate the human necessity for a feeling of
efficacy, the human need to make a difference, is to touch
the depths of the wisdom of Alcoholics Anonymous.
Precisely here, A.A. taps one of the few unchanging facets
of the essence of the human condition. Ponder, for example,
in this context of how A.A. works, this insight (again Laing's)
into the nature of the thirst of modern mankind:

Every human being, whether child or adult,
seems to require *significance,* that is *place in
another person's world*...It seems to be a universal
human desire to wish to occupy a place in the
world of at least one other person. Perhaps the
greatest solace in religion is in the sense that one
lives in the Presence of an Other.[34]

Mutuality means making a difference by giving *and* getting: one both gets by giving and gives by getting. This reciprocal conjunction of the experience of giving and the experience of receiving characterizes not only Alcoholics Anonymous, but all expressions of human love. This reality of love is one deep reason why Alcoholics Anonymous works.

> We ourselves want to be needed. We do not only have needs, we are also strongly motivated by *neededness*...We are restless when we are not needed, because we feel "unfinished," "incomplete," and we can only get completed in and through these relationships. We are motivated to search not only for what we lack and need but also for that for which we are needed, what is wanted from us.[35]

Honesty with self and others

The second mutuality taught by and put into practice within Alcoholics Anonymous involves honesty. One vivid lesson of A.A.'s experience is that there exists an essential mutuality between honesty with self and honesty with others: both may be present or both may be absent, but neither can exist without the other. Most members of Alcoholics Anonymous come to their understanding of the necessary mutuality between honesty with self and with others precisely from their personal experience of the inevitable mutuality of dishonesty with self and others.

> Those who deceive themselves are obliged to deceive others. It is impossible for me to maintain a false picture of myself unless I falsify your picture of yourself and me.[36]

> ...it is a form of self-deception to suppose that one can say one thing and think another.[37]

As with the mutuality of making a difference, of giving
and getting, the mutuality involved in honesty and
dishonesty with self and others is not a unique discovery of
Alcoholics Anonymous. The most profound description of
the process underlying this mutuality has been offered by
the research psychoanalyst who has been called "the poet-
philosopher of the current human condition," Dr. Leslie H.
Farber. His insight merits quotation at length, for it captures
a theme heard often in the personal histories narrated at
meetings of Alcoholics Anonymous.

> As a child grows gradually aware of the absolute
> separateness of his being from all others in the
> world, he discovers that this condition offers both
> pleasure and terror ... To the extent that he must
> — or believes that he must — toy with his own
> presentation of himself to others to earn the
> attention and approval he craves ..., he will
> experience a queer, unnamable apprehension ...
> This uneasy state is both painful and corrupting.
>
> It is commonly believed that this pain and
> corruption are consequences of his low self-esteem
> and fear of others' indifference and rejection, that
> these cause him to project himself falsely. It seems
> more likely that once this habit begins to harden,
> the crucial source of pain *is* his corruption. In his
> constant inability or unwillingness to tell the truth
> about who he is, he knows himself in his heart to
> be faking.
>
> Not merely is he ashamed of having and
> harboring a secret, unlovely, illegitimate self. The
> spiritual burden of not appearing as the person he
> "is," or not "being" the person he appears to be —
> the extended and deliberate confusion of seeming
> and being — is by and large intolerable if held in

direct view. If the integrity he craves is to be
denied him, at least he will have its illusion. If he
cannot publicize his private self, . . . then he will
command his private self to conform to the public
one. This beguiles to a *loss* of truth; not only
"telling" it, but *knowing* it.

There are some things it is impossible both to do
and at the same time to impersonate oneself
doing. Speaking truthfully is one of them.[38]

There is, thus, a mutuality between honesty with self and
honesty with others: it is necessary to avoid self-deception if
one is to be honest with others, but at the same time one
must be honest with others if one is to avoid self-deception.
The drinking alcoholic, if he glimpses this realization at all,
finds in it only the most vicious of circles. One gift of A.A.'s
insight is the revelation that this mutuality can enhance
growth rather than hasten self-destruction. How to live its
paradoxical wisdom becomes, for the sober alcoholic, an
essential part of his continuing participation in Alcoholics
Anonymous as both fellowship and program.

Dependence and independence

Both mutualities already examined — making a difference
and honesty — flow into the third mutuality inherent in A.A.
therapy: that between dependence and independence. Here
also, A.A.'s insight into the essential connection between
personal dependence and personal independence derives
from its central focus on the reality of essential limitation as
the first truth of the human condition. It is because the
human is somehow the juncture of the infinite with the
limited — because to be human is to be both angel and
beast — that human dependence and human independence
must be mutually related, not only between people but
within each person. Mutuality means that each enables and

fulfills the other. To speak of a mutuality between human dependence and human independence, then, is to point out not only that *both* are necessary within human experience, but also that *each* — dependence and independence — becomes fully human and humanizing only by connection with the other.

Most other therapies — therapies are not infused with the philosophy of Alcoholics Anonymous — tend to accept the alcoholic's denial of limitation and therefore to interpret personal dependence and personal independence as contradictory rather than enhancing. Their goal of independence is not unrelated to their ideal of objectivity and their hope of curing. Yet, as we saw in our treatment of the A.A. goals of limited control and limited dependence, the alcoholic gains the freedom to not-drink only by acknowledging that his problem is not *"dependence* on alcohol," but "dependence on *alcohol."* The experience of Alcoholics Anonymous suggests that dependence is no more "cured" than is alcoholism: rather, the alcoholic's dependence comes to be healed — to be integrated into his whole personality in a way that enhances his humanity — by the mutuality of caring.

For specific reasons within the history of psychological thought, the study of continuing human dependence has not found a central place in any theory of human development.[39] Recently, however, this surprising lacuna has begun to be filled. At least one school of analytic psychiatry has achieved rare success by building on the fundamental insight: "Dependence *versus* independence is the basic neurotic conflict."[40] According to Donald Winnicott, one leader of this school of thought that has given rise to "personal relationship therapy," for the truly mature person, "dependence and independence do not become conflicting issues, rather they are complementary."

The truly mature person, that is, experiences "ontological security." For the individual whose own being becomes secured in the primary experiential sense, relatedness with others is potentially gratifying and fulfilling. The "ontologically insecure person," on the contrary, one who has not come to terms with the complementary of dependence and independence, is pre-occupied with preserving rather than fulfilling self: he becomes obsessed with the task of preventing himself from losing himself. Such an ontologically insecure person reaches out to others in self-seeking dependency, out of the same needs that drive the alcoholic or addict to seek chemical relief. Ontological insecurity undermines any possibility of true mutuality.

The implicit philosophical psychology of Alcoholics Anonymous reflects these insights. A.A. provides, in fact, a model for maturity that adds to this line of thought; for the implicit A.A. paradigm specifies how the older, unsatisfactory developmental schema for human growth can be transcended. The A.A. insight, deriving from the fellowship's historical rejection of absolutes and consistent emphasis on essential limitation, focuses attention on the essential *some*-ness of the human experience.

Classic therapies analyze and explore the first two steps in human development and strive to raise their clients to a third stage. In their understanding, the newborn infant comes into the world claiming by its actions a grandiose omnipotence. Its very literal cries are designed to enforce the demand, "I am God." Within the first year of life, however, reality impinges upon the newly conscious infant. Becoming aware of its very real separation from its mother — of her other-ness and the infant's own consequence absolute dependence upon that separate "other" — the baby veers to the opposite extreme and begins living the implicit plaint of childhood, "I am nothing."

Maturity is attained, according to the usual therapeutic assumptions about human development, when the individual can accept and affirm: "I am something." It is here that Alcoholics Anonymous implicitly suggests that the process of growth into truly mature adulthood can contain one more phase — indeed that, at least for alcoholics, it must. The memory of their experience and their thinking processes while drinking does not allow sober members of Alcoholics Anonymous to rest in the proclamation, "I am something"; for the inherent insatiability of the self-centeredness that is the root of his troubles leads the alcoholic to accent the first or to add to the last syllable of that then-no-longer simple affirmation. "I am something" or "I am something *else*" betokens not the simple affirmation of self-acceptance, but instead a self-centered exceptionalism. This self-centered exceptionalism not only expresses a demand that denies essential limitation but also imposes on the one so demanding the further demand for alcohol to sustain that grandiose inflation. The alcoholic, at least, cannot rest comfortably anywhere near the essentially adolescent condition that affirms, "I am something."

Implicitly, then, A.A. suggests to its members a fourth stage, a further growth. The self-accepting affirmation of the truly sober alcoholic must become: "I am someone." This statement reflects more accurately human reality as essentially limited and opens to the acceptance of both self and others as persons who are subjects. Its final term invites a double accent, and thus forecloses the possibility of any too great emphasis upon the "I." The acceptance and affirmation of *some*-ness closes the door to either infantile claim of "all' or "nothing." The embrace and cherishing of *one*-ness invites to the joyous pluralism of complementarity that is the essential dynamic of Alcoholics Anonymous: the shared honesty of mutual vulnerability openly acknowledged.

The concept of "*some-one*-ness" again reveals the inherently mutual nature of the existential human condition. One whose wholeness consists in essential limitation cannot be either wholly dependent *or* wholly independent: to be human is to be both independent and dependent, and because both, neither totally. One can only be both; one cannot only be either; and because one can have only both, one's possession of each is intrinsically limited. Because, for human beings, reality is essentially bound up with limitation, one achieves true independence only by also acknowledging real dependence. Similarly, one can be dependent in a truly human way only by also exercising real independence. Independence is enabled and enriched by dependence just as our waking hours can be fruitful only if we obtain adequate sleep. Likewise, constructive dependence requires independence just as healthy sleep requires adequate waking exercise. The very rhythms of human life reflect the mutuality inherent in human nature.

In a sense one "charges batteries" by dependence, thus enabling independent operation. The reverse of the analogy proves equally true: being dependent without exercising independence is like over-charging a battery rarely used — destructive of both the self and the source. The weakness of the analogy, of course, lies in its implicit "either-or" sequence. In human reality, dependence and independence do not so much alternate as reciprocate — occur at the same time, mutually reinforcing each other.

Alcoholics Anonymous, both in its suggestion of a "Higher Power" and in the way its meetings work, invites and enables the living out of this mutuality between human dependence and personal independence. The First Step of the A.A. program establishes the foundation for this understanding: only by acknowledging continuing dependence upon alcohol does the A.A. member achieve the continuing independence of freedom from addiction to alcohol. This mutuality between dependence and independence also clarifies — because it undergirds — A.A.'s emphasis on limited control and limited dependence, topics explored earlier. These are, we now see more clearly, not two separate concepts, but obverse sides of the one coin of essential human limitation. Because of essential limitation, to be fully human requires the acknowledgment of both limited control and limited dependence; and the embrace of *each* is necessary to the attainment of its apparent opposite.

PART FOUR: CONCLUSION

I. BEING "BOTH": THE NATURE OF FREEDOM

Any true therapy for shame must acknowledge and accept the necessary mutualities that flow from the essential limitation of the human condition. "Others" — other self-aware essentially limited individuals — have a twofold role in such a therapy: (1) their example facilitates the acceptance of one's own limitation; (2) their presence enables a degree of transcendence of limitation, for they invite living the mutualities of making a difference, honesty, and dependence-independence.

Shame contains a "not" — the *not* imposed by essential limitation. To be human is to be aware that one falls short. To be human is to know that the ability to be is also the ability to be not. Thus, to be human is to feel shame — to feel "bad" about and "to blame" for the not-ness lodged in one's essence. Why this "feeling to blame"? Because of the anomalous nature of the human as not-God, as beast-angel, as essentially limited yet craving unlimitedness. The anomaly is inherent, for to be human is to be "both-and" rather than "either-or." Confronted with the task of being human, one must live *both* its polarities: one cannot be only either. The shame of "feeling to blame" arises from the necessary imperfection of such both-ness: inevitably one falls short of being either beast or angel — neither can be total so long as both are actual.

Within Alcoholics Anonymous, the recovering alcoholic comes to learn that there exists a necessary equation — connection — between being limited and being real. The practice of mutuality inculcates the truths that to be real is to be limited, and that to be limited is to be real. This necessary fact of the human condition is perhaps clearest in the matter of freedom. The drinking alcoholic turned to alcohol in search of freedom; the recovering alcoholic searches for freedom from alcohol. In the A.A. understanding, the second search will prove as vain as the first, unless the alcoholic learns the simple truth that to be human is to be both free and unfree — that neither can be absolute.

The recovering alcoholic learns first in Alcoholics Anonymous that his freedom, although real, is limited — and that his freedom, although limited, is real. Free to drink, the alcoholic is not free to not drink. To attain the freedom to not drink, the alcoholic accepts limitation of his freedom to drink. But this realization, important as it is, does not suffice for true, joyous sobriety. The alcoholic in recovery must come to see, however, hazily, that this acceptance is not a concession. The word "although," that is to say, must be replaced by the affirmation "because": because real, freedom is limited; because limited, freedom is real.

A.A. experience continually reminds the recovering alcoholic how the apparently unlimited freedom to drink inevitably leads to increasing bondage and ever greater losses of freedom (to work, to love and to be loved, to live).

The same A.A. experience progressively reveals, on the other hand, how the limited freedom to not drink brings in its wake ever increasing freedoms. The recovering alcoholic within Alcoholics Anonymous thus learns a profound truth: with freedom as with any other human phenomenon, to be real is to be limited, for limitation proves reality. This understanding enables both joyous acceptance of the human condition and true recovery from alcoholic addiction. It enables these "both" because, at depth, that acceptance and that recovery are one and the same.

II. PLURALISM, TOLERANCE, COMPLEMENTARITY, AND LOVE

This is the profound lesson of Alcoholics Anonymous, the deep truth that A.A. both teaches and enables: creative acceptance of the reality of essential human limitation. That acceptance is the core of the program and the fellowship of Alcoholics Anonymous. Continuing our analysis of how A.A. utilizes this insight requires two additional concepts: pluralism and complementarity. Each is a corollary that clarifies the practical implications of human essential limitation.

Pluralism means accepting that, among those essentially limited, there can be no *one* way of being that is perfect or "best." "Easy Does It," cautions A.A.: "Live and Let Live." Complementarity implies that imperfect beings can aid in completing or fulfilling each other. The "experience, strength, and hope" of each alcoholic enhances the experience, strength, and hope of every other alcoholic within A.A.

Alcoholics Anonymous enables and promotes — indeed thrives on — pluralistic complementarity because each A.A. member not only accepts limitation but finds in that very limitation ("I am an alcoholic") the basis for relating to others within A.A. Thus members of Alcoholics Anonymous remain always aware of the possibility and necessity of mutuality, of giving and getting. Because their mutuality derives so consciously from shared weakness (their alcoholism), A.A. members give and get without threat: alike in weakness, they find in their differences only strength.

Alcoholics Anonymous arrived at its acceptance of pluralism honestly. The insight, and its implications, were at first uncongenial to a fellowship whose members were characterized by obsessive-compulsive behavior — alcoholics who, as co-founder Bill Wilson never tired of reminding, tended by their nature to be "all-or-nothing people." Yet Alcoholics Anonymous, largely through Bill Wilson, learned the lesson of pluralistic tolerance from early on:

> In the early days of A.A. I spent a lot of time trying to get people to agree with me, to practice A.A. principles as I did, and so forth. For so long as I did this . . . A.A. grew very slowly.[41]
>
> A.A. works for people with *differing* views — that is *good.*[42]
>
> Honesty gets us sober but tolerance keeps us sober.[43]

Very early in A.A. history, indeed, Wilson intuited and skillfully inculcated the unshakeable basis for the fellowship's tolerance of even apparent perversity as well as of every diversity:

> The way our "worthy" alcoholics have sometimes tried to judge the "less worthy" is, as we look back on it, rather comical. Imagine, if you can, one alcoholic judging another![44]

Tolerance thus flows naturally from A.A.'s central focus on human essential limitation. Because human beings are essentially limited, any individual's possession of truth must be — like anyone's claim to freedom — limited, if it is real. In fostering such tolerance, Alcoholics Anonymous teaches and promotes not only an openness to pluralism that accepts difference, but the sense of complementarity that welcomes and values diversity. ". . . tolerance keeps us sober" because finding value in others' distinctness — in others as others who are persons rather than objects — reminds not only of the alcoholic's essential not-God-ness, but that for the alcoholic strength arises out of weakness.

Because of the essential limitation of human existence, because of the mixed nature of the human condition as not-God, as beast-angel, as essentially limited yet craving "more," each human being is incomplete. Because of this incompleteness, each needs others. Because of this essential incompleteness, indeed, each person most clearly discovers and reveals his own nature by the particular ways in which he needs other essentially limited human beings.

Because any "other" is also essentially incomplete, any constructive human relationship is characterized by complementarity — the sense that each fulfills the other. Complementarity, because it accepts and is founded on the essential limitation of both, involves acknowledgment and acceptance by each of the other as other who is also person, and therefore as concrete, unique, different, potentially enriching individual. This awareness of complementarity opens to the mutual sense of mutual fulfillment. The sense of complementarity consists in the realization that the existence of both is affirmed by each other, that the differences of each enrich rather than threaten the other.

This understanding reflects the model of love hymned throughout the ages by poets and philosophers: biological heterosexuality, the complementarity of male and female. Most obviously in this prototype, love — the mutuality of giving and receiving that enhances and fulfills — flourishes because of difference rather than despite it. Alcoholics Anonymous teaches love because love itself derives from the acceptance of essential human limitation. The denial of essential limitation renders love impossible, for denying limitation and therefore rejecting complementarity leads to demanding in "love" only likeness — a demand that results either in narcissism or in the destructive attempt to impose likeness, and neither of these can be love. The pluralistic insight, the kind of tolerance that derives from the acceptance of essential limitation, on the other hand, finds difference enriching rather than threatening: it thus opens to the love that flourishes not despite difference, but because of it.

Recognizing, admitting, and accepting essential limitation can be terrifying. Consciousness of essential limitation can raise the defenses that wall off others and therefore preclude love. But it need not, as the experience of Alcoholics Anonymous testifies. Members of Alcoholics Anonymous seem not only to grasp but to improve upon the maxim of Goethe: "Against the superiority [*difference*] of another person there is no other remedy but love.["][45]

Enlarging the possibilities of mutuality—of pluralism and complementarity—requires risk. Expanding the scope of mutual love depends upon risking exposure: the honesty that reveals essential limitation and thus admits need must confront shame. The program and fellowship of Alcoholics Anonymous enable such risk and confrontation by inculcating the qualities of hope and trust that permit truly free choice. Accepting contingency (not-God-ness) equips one to survive and even to flourish in a world of possibility. Such acceptance cures addiction, in the sense that it reveals addiction's inherent untruth.

Whenever the desire for emotional security
becomes primary over all else, for whatever
reason, addiction sets in... Because he is so
vulnerable, what the addict is ideally striving for is
perfect invulnerability. He only gives himself in
exchange for the promise of safety.[46]
But there is no absolute safety, for the human condition
admits of neither perfection nor invulnerability. Alcoholics
Anonymous teaches this, but also more. A.A. both inspires
and furnishes the answer to what might be called "the
alcoholic's meditation on honesty, pain, and shame."

Honesty involves exposure: the exposure of self-
as-feared that leads to the discovery of self-as-is.
Both of these selves are essentially vulnerable: to
be is to be able to hurt and to be hurt. But
something tells us that we should not hurt: that we
should neither hurt others nor hurt within
ourselves. Yet we do—both hurt and hurt, both
cause and feel pain.

When we cause pain, we experience guilt; when
we feel pain, we suffer shame. The pain, the hurt,
the guilt of the first is overt: it exists outside of us,
"objectively." The pain, the hurt, the shame of the
second is hidden: it gnaws within, it is
"subjective." Neither can be healed without
confronting the other. A bridge is needed—a
connection between the hurt that we cause and
the hurt that we are.

That bridge cannot be built alone. The honesty
that is its foundation must be shared. A bridge
cannot have only one end. Without sharing, there
can be no bridge. But a bridge needs a span as
well as foundations. This bridge's span is
vulnerability—the capacity to be wounded, the

ability to know hurt. "I need" because "I hurt" — if
deepest need is honest. What I need is another's
hurt, another's need. Such a need on my part
would be "sick" — if the other had not the same
need of me, of my hurt and my need. Because we
share hurt, we can share healing. Because we know
need, we can heal each other.

Our mutual healing will be not the healing of
curing, but the healing of caring. To heal is to
make whole. Curing makes whole from the
outside: it is good healing, but it cannot touch my
deepest need, my deepest hurt — my shame, the
dread of myself that I harbor within. Caring makes
whole from within: it reconciles me to myself-as-I-
am — not-God, beast-angel, *human*. Caring enables
me to touch the joy of living that is the other side
of my shame, of my not-God-ness, of my
humanity.

But I can care, can become whole, only if you
care enough — need enough — to share your shame
with me.

Could the same be true for you?

NOTES AND BIBLIOGRAPHY

1. [William Griffith Wilson], "The Fellowship of Alcoholics Anonymous," in *Alcohol, Science and Society* (New Haven: Yale Univ. Press, 1945), p. 472.
2. On the Self-Help Mutual Aid Group Movement, cf. especially Leonard D. Borman (ed.), *Explorations in Self-Help and Mutual Aid* (Evanston, IL: Northwestern Univ., 1975); Gerald Caplan and Marie Killilea (eds.), *Support Systems and Mutual Help: Multidisciplinary Explorations* (New York: Grune and Stratton, 1976); Alan Gartner and Frank Riessman, *Self-Help in the Human Services* (San Francisco: Jossey-Bass, 1977); Frank Riessman and Alan Gartner, *Help: A Working Guide to Self-Help Groups* (Watts, 1979).
3. Ernest Kurtz, "Why It Works: The Intellectual Significance of Alcoholics Anonymous," *Journal of Studies on Alcohol, Forthcoming.*
4. Cf. Helen Merrell Lynd, *On Shame and the Search for Identity* (New York: Harcourt, Brace, & World, 1958), pp. 35-36.
5. Cf. Lynd, *On Shame,* pp. 24-26.
6. Cf. William Barrett, *Irrational Man* (New York: Doubleday, 1958), pp. 225-227.
7. Cf. Ernest Kurtz, *Not-God: A History of Alcoholics Anonymous* (Center City, MN: Hazelden, 1979), index listings for "Oxford Group" and "Four Absolutes."
8. Letters in which Bill Wilson used this phrase or "spiritual kindergarten" include to Caryl Chessman, 3 May 1954; to Dr. Tom P., 4 April 1955; to Walter B., 1 July 1958; to Father K., 28 July 1958; to Betty L., 8 December 1967.
9. *Alcoholics Anonymous* (A.A. World Services, Inc.: New York, 1976 rev. ed.), pp. 58-60.
10. Cf. Kurtz, "Why It Works."

11. Quoted by Lucien Goldmann, *The Hidden God* (New York: Humanities Press, 1964), p. 188.

12. Quoted by Morton and Lucia White, *The Intellectual Versus the City* (New York: Mentor, 1964), p. 188.

13. Ernest Becker, *The Denial of Death* (New York: Free Press, 1973), p. 58.

14. Cf. Lynd, *On Shame,* pp. 94-96, 145-147.

15. On alcoholism as a metaphor for the human condition, cf. Kurtz, *Not-God,* pp. 200-202.

16. Wilson (New York) to Howard C., 15 November 1960; to Patricia N., 7 January 1963; to Bob C., 23 June 1964.

17. The original wording of A.A.'s Seventh Step may be found in the "Pre-Publication (Multilith) Copy of the Big Book (1939)": *Alcoholic's Anonymous* (Newark, NJ: Works Publishing, 1939), p. 26.

18. Cf. Helen Block Lewis, *Shame and Guilt in Neurosis* (New York: International Universities Press, 1971), pp. 81, 84.

19. On the "disease-concept," cf. E. M. Jellinek, *The Disease Concept of Alcoholism* (New Haven: College and Univ. Press, 1960); also Mark Keller, "The Disease Concept of Alcoholism Revisited," *Journal of Studies on Alcohol* 37: 1674-1717 (1976), Cf. also Kurtz, *Not-God,* pp. 22-23, on A.A.'s use of "malady."

20. Cf. Lynd, *On Shame,* pp. 40, 64, 235.

21. *Alcoholics Anonymous* (1976 ed.), p. 62.

22. H. J. Almond, "Moral Re-Armament: The Oxford Group," unpublished Master's thesis, Yale University, 1947, p. 12.

23. *Twelve Steps and Twelve Traditions* (New York: A.A. World Services, Inc., 1978), pp. 57, 62. Note that in this "Sixteenth Printing, February 1978," the pagination differs from earlier printings, in which these quotations appeared on pp. 59 and 63.

24. Cf. Lynd, *On Shame,* pp. 27-32; the excerpt from Maugham appears on pp. 29-30.

25. Cf., for this idea and its exploration, David G. Edwards, "Shame and Pain and 'Shut up or I'll Really Give You Something to Cry About,'" *Clinical Social Work Journal* 4: 3-13 (1976); for the quotations in the next paragraph, 7-12.

26. Harry M. Tiebout, "The Act of Surrender in the Therapeutic Process," *Quarterly Journal of Studies on Alcohol* 10: 48-58 (1959); "Surrender Versus Compliance in Therapy," *QJSA* 14:58-68 (1963).

27. Stanton Peele (with Archie Brodsky), *Love and Addiction* (New York: Taplinger, 1975), p. 232.

28. Francis T. Chambers, Jr., "Analysis and Comparison of Three Treatment Measures for Alcoholism: Antabuse, the Alcoholics Anonymous Approach, and Psychotherapy," *British Journal of Addiction* 50: 29-41 (1953).

29. William Glasser, *The Identity Society* (New York: Harper and Row Perennial, 1976), p. 58.

30. Lynd, *On Shame,* pp. 159-160.

31. *Alcoholics Anonymous* (1976 ed.), p. 185.

32. R. D. Laing, *Self and Others* (Baltimore: Pelican, 1971), pp. 84-85.

33. Laing, *Self and Others,* p. 138.

34. Laing, *Self and Others,* p. 136.

35. Andras Angyal, quoted by Milton Mayeroff, *On Caring* (New York: Harper & Row Perennial, 1971), frontispiece.

36. Laing, *Self and Others,* p. 143.

37. R.D. Laing, *The Divided Self* (Baltimore: Penguin, 1965), p. 18.

38. Leslie H. Farber, *Lying, Despair, Jealousy, Envy, Sex, Suicide, Drugs, and the Good Life* (New York: Basic Books, 1976), pp. 196-198.

39. A brief summary of this point may be found in Willard Gaylin, "In The Beginning," in Gaylin *et al, Doing Good:*

The Limits of Benevolence (New York: Pantheon, 1978), pp. 12 ff.

40. This line of thought is best summarized in Harry Guntrip, *Psychoanalytic Theory, Therapy, and the Self* (New York: Basic Books, 1971); cf. especially, and for the quotations here, pp. 115, 118, 126, 190.
41. Wilson (New York) to May M., 24 August 1964.
42. Wilson (New York) to John G., 9 October 1967.
43. [Wilson], "The Fellowship of Alcoholics Anonymous," in *Alcohol, Science and Society* (New Haven: Yale University Press, 1945), p. 472.
44. [Wilson], "Who is a Member of Alcoholics Anonymous — By Bill," *The A.A. Grapevine* 3:3 (August 1946), 3.
45. *Gegen grosse Vorzuge eines andern gibt es kein rettungsmittel als die Liebe:* Johann Wolfgang Goethe, *Gedenkausgabe Der Werke, Briefe Und Gesprache* (Zurich: Ernst Beutler, 1949), p. 176; a translation may be found in Johann Wolfgang von Goethe, *Elective Affinities,* tr. Elizabeth Mayer and Louise Bogan (Chicago: Henry Regnery, 1963), p. 191.
46. Peele, *Love and Addiction,* pp. 111, 87.